SHERI JEAN SCHMITT

LIFE'S EMOTIONS
AND
PERSONAL CARE
WITH
PEANUT

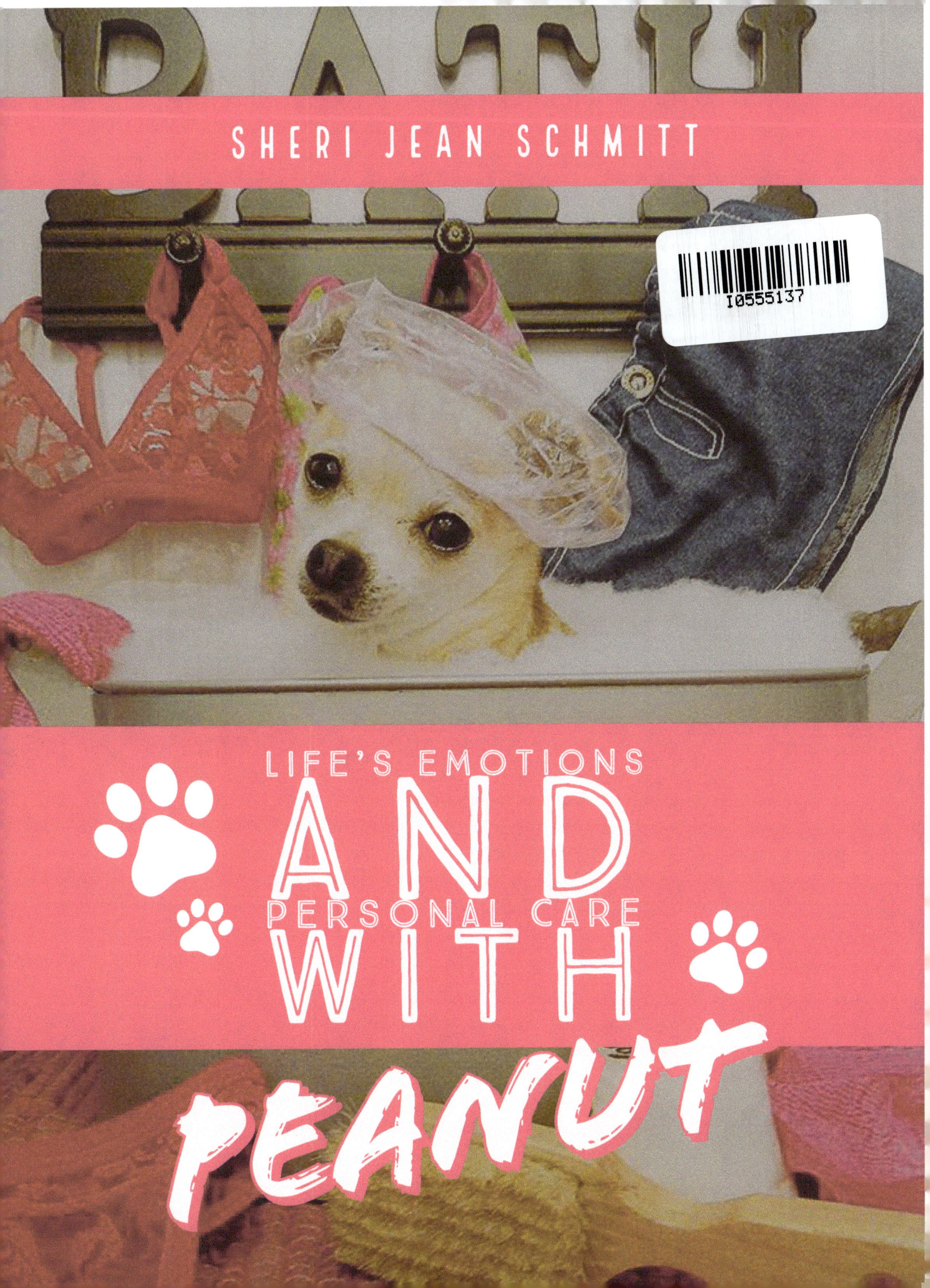

I0555137

Life's Emotions and Personal Care with Peanut
Copyright © 2025 by Sheri Jean Schmitt

All rights reserved. No part of this publication may be reproduced, distributed, or transmitted in any form or by any means, including photocopying, recording, or other electronic or mechanical methods, without the prior written permission of the author, except in the case of brief quotations embodied in critical reviews and certain other non-commercial uses permitted by copyright law.

ISBN
978-1-969642-12-8 (Paperback)
978-1-969642-11-1 (eBook)
978-1-969642-13-5 (Hardcover)

Contents

Freedom

Love For Country

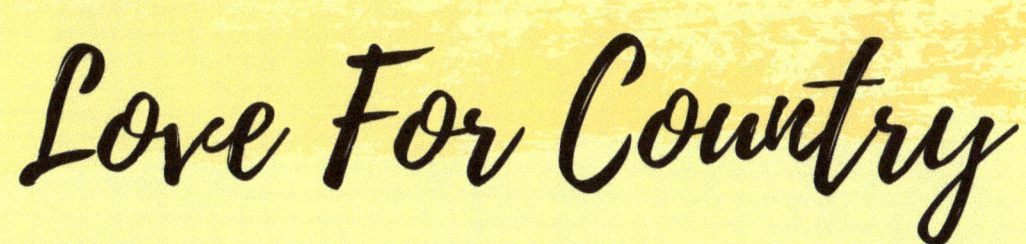

Love For Country

Here I am as an actor. I play an angel in a Broadway musical. I love New York City very much. When I have time off from performing, I go out and explore the city. I have to check out the red fire hydrants everywhere I go. The city lights at night are the most wonderful sight. It seems so magical.

I like taking walks in Central Park with my friend, Caesar. When we need a break, we find a park bench to sit. As we rest, we watch the horse drawn carriages go by. At the park, we also have fun chasing the pigeons and squirrels. Mr. Black Bird likes to swoop down at us from the sky. Yikes! We run and hide!

Seeing the Statue of Liberty makes me pause. I feel thankful for living in such a great country. Where there is freedom, your spirit soars. You can use your imagination. You can be the best at what you love. And, yes, even make mistakes and fail along the way. You can be anything you want with hard work and determination. Don't get scared now!

Looking Good Inside and Out

The beauty salon makes me look good and feel pretty. When I feel good on the outside, I feel good on the inside. When I take care of myself, it gives me confidence. I work hard at my passions in life and this too gives me confidence. Do your best, even if you fail. Know humility, and do what's right, even if it's not in your favor. When you have confidence, you can do anything. Be true to yourself!

At the salon, I have my hair curled and then get a pedicure. I catch up on fashion and beauty ideas from the fashion magazines while waiting for my hair to get done. Naturally, I will have to get pink polish on my nails. I look fabulous!

PEANUT'S WINTER WONDERLAND

PEANUT'S WINTER WONDERLAND

All bundled up for Winter. Wearing boots keeps my paws warm. My fur, hooded jacket keeps my head warm. Shhh! Don't tell anyone, but I have long underwear on for warmth too.

Cold weather is for activities such as skating, sledding, and snowball fights. For me, snow mobiling down the trails is my favorite. A group of us usually go. It's fun that way. We make stops along the way to warm up, get something to eat, and sit and visit. Fun time! My second favorite thing to do is to ride horses at night under a bright moon. Light reflects off the snow so it's easy to see. It's really still at night. I feel like I'm the only dog on earth.

I always look forward to laying in front of the fireplace in my dog bed. Watching the fire dance and listening to the crackling sounds is very soothing. Good night!

Spa Day

relax

It puts me in calming state mind.

seize the day

Spa Day

Going to the spa to get a massage is relaxing for the body. I especially like my paws massaged. It's good for the mind too. It puts you in a calming state of mind. I don't even think about the neighbor's Doberman dog barking at me all the time. He's scary!

Getting a mud bath makes my fur very soft. I get paw cream on my paws and ear drops in my ears. I leave feeling like a new dog. Aaahh!

I'm ready for dog walks and Frisbee catching in the park. I also meet up with my dog pals there. We love chasing each other and play tug of war with a rope. We never forget to keep watch of our dog masters so they stay safe. We wouldn't want anyone or anything to hurt them. Life is good as a dog! Dogs rule! Get out there and give your very best and keep your ears clean.

seize the day

DOWN TIME

Down Time

Down time is important because it rejuvenates body and mind. All work and no play makes Peanut a dull dog. Enjoy your work but work hard. Know when to stop and smell the biscuits.

On my down time, I enjoy motorcycling with Caesar. We go for weekend road trips. I also enjoy painting portraits of my friends and riding a horse.

Find what your joys are. Fun and laughter is the best medicine. Use your imagination. Dreams and insperations widen your mind and brings opportunities for you, so use it. When your homework is done, what do you do for fun on your down time?

What do you think of my motorcycle outfit? My jacket keeps me warm. The bandana keeps wind out of my ears. I think I look pretty tough, don't you?

See ya!

BATH TIME

Taking time out to wash my fur. I get very dirty from all my adventures. It's very busy work being a dog. Dogs protect our owners. We are companions, we are friends, and we are also there for support. Some of my pals work for the police, search and rescue teams, and even the military.

Bathing outside in a tub is fun. Oh my! I hope no one sees me! I scrub all my nooks and crannies. Wearing a shower cap keeps the water out of my ears. I use the brush to scrub my back and paws. Ooohh! That feels good!

I like lots of suds in the tub. With the suds, I put a beard on my nose and a big poof of suds on my head. I look like Abraham Lincoln, who was the 16th president of the United States. He was known as "Honest Abe" because he valued honesty. I will call myself, "Honest Peanut the Dog." Always remember—honesty is the best policy!

WEENIE'S NEW HOME

"Smile even when you don't feel happy and after awhile you will be happy for real."

WEENIE'S NEW HOME

Weenie is an actress. She is in the TV series, Dog Nose Best. In the show, she owns a dog motel. A dog motel is a place where the human dog owners drop off their dogs while going on vacation. The show follows the lives of the motel guests and Weenie showing her quick wit.

Weenie bought her first home with all her hard work. You too can work hard towards a goal. With hard work, sacrifice, and determination, all things are possible. In life, you may have many ups and downs to get to your goals, but stay focused on the prize. Never give up. Always push forward. Nothing is guaranteed. Give life your all. You will feel good that you tried everything to be successful. Weenie's secret to life is to always be positive, no matter what. Weenie says, "Smile even when you don't feel happy and after awhile you will be happy for real." Smile because people aren't attracted to grumpy-grumps!

SQUEKS

SQUEKS

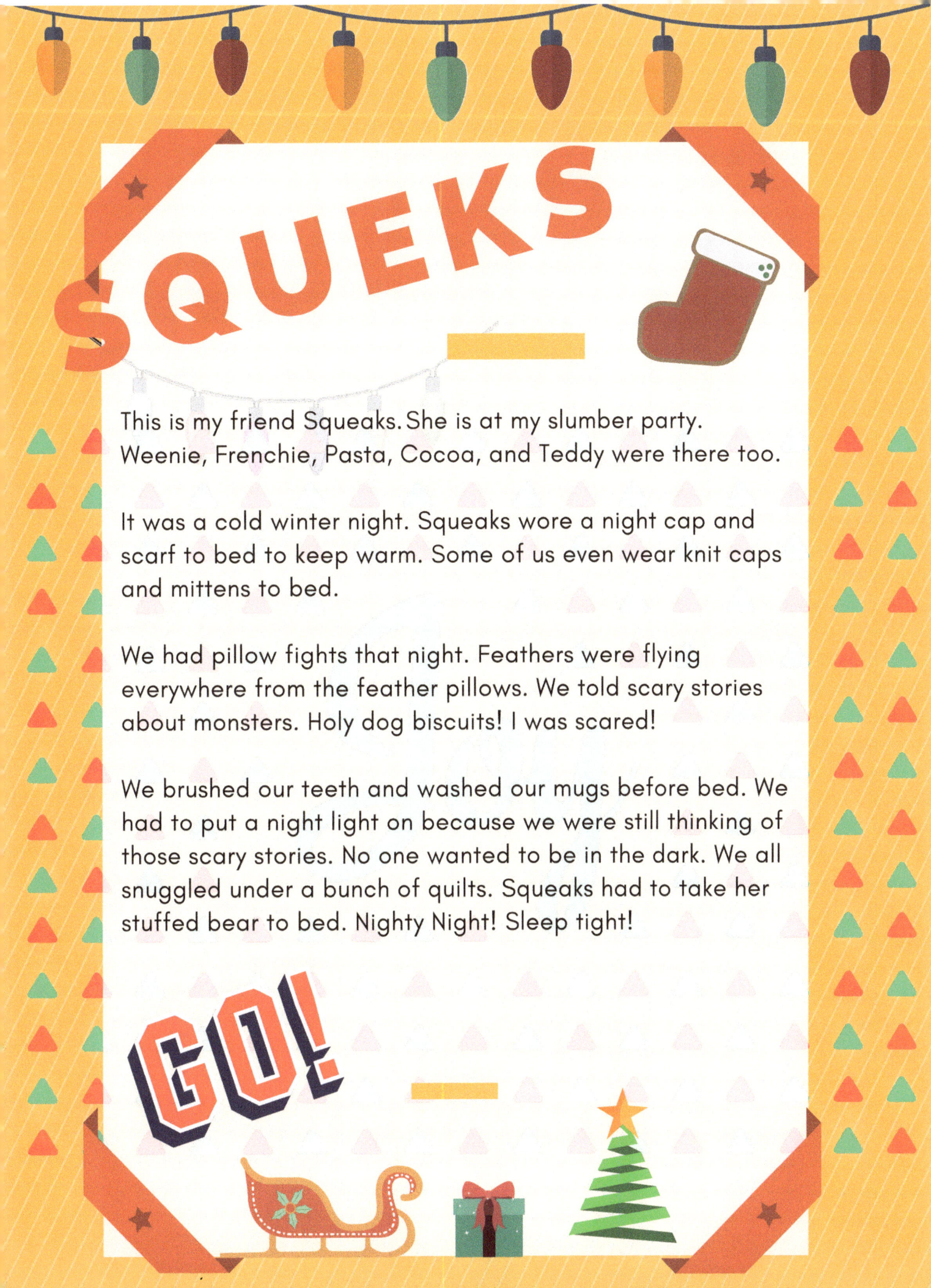

This is my friend Squeaks. She is at my slumber party. Weenie, Frenchie, Pasta, Cocoa, and Teddy were there too.

It was a cold winter night. Squeaks wore a night cap and scarf to bed to keep warm. Some of us even wear knit caps and mittens to bed.

We had pillow fights that night. Feathers were flying everywhere from the feather pillows. We told scary stories about monsters. Holy dog biscuits! I was scared!

We brushed our teeth and washed our mugs before bed. We had to put a night light on because we were still thinking of those scary stories. No one wanted to be in the dark. We all snuggled under a bunch of quilts. Squeaks had to take her stuffed bear to bed. Nighty Night! Sleep tight!

GO!

Laundry

From my travels I have much laundry to do. Playing in the mud is fun, but necessary to clean up afterwards. I use plenty of soap to get the dirt out.

I use a scrub board to clean my clothes, which was invented in 1797. I think it's time I upgrade to a
washing machine. The washing machine was invented in 1851. Thank goodness for inventors. They make our lives better with their inventions. Always push yourself to learn more because maybe you will invent something one day. Never settle for being average!

As I hang the clothes outside on the clothesline, I hear the birds singing! Gee whiz, I hope they don't poop on the clothes. Washed clothes that have been hanging outside to dry take on the smell of the fresh country air. Sniff, sniff. Aaaaah! Hope no one sees my underwear!

I'M PROUD OF YOU

I'M PROUD OF YOU

My good friend Squeaks is very photogenic. She has been on the cover of several dog magazines. She poses in photos for the greeting card company, Barking Dog Cards. This is one of those photos. She is currently doing work for dog catalogs, modeling the latest dog clothes. The hottest color of the year is pink. Sweaters are a big seller. The look of the wild is what's trending. Leopard print is seen everywhere.

I'm proud of Squeaks. She works very hard. She goes out of her way to help others. You also can strive to make your parents proud. Be the best you can be. Do what your parents tell you and they will be proud.

Hugs and kisses to my forever friend, Squeaks!
XOXOXO

SOPHIE

Grateful

SOPHIE

This is Sophie. She is my friend's mother. Weenie gave her mom the gift of a salon treatment for Mother's Day. Mother's Day is a day you honor your mother for all she means to you. Your mother does much for you, so she gets her own day to feel special. Be grateful for your mother every day!

Sophie wanted her hair curled with a big bow put on the top of her head. She also wanted her tail blown out fluffy. Oh my! Whiskers trimmed and nail polish was a must.

Weenie took her mom out to eat after her makeover. They went to Wags and Licks Restaurant to have dog biscuits and gravy.

Weenie and Sophie had a wonderful day out. They ended the day in pajamas and slippers. Sitting down With a bowl of warm milk, they watched the show, Jake the Pitt Bull Detective. He solves cases of lost and stolen dogs. Oooh! Watch out!

POSITIVE VIBES

Peanut & Caeser's Wedding

Our wedding day! Our dog family and puppy friends came to celebrate our big day. We had a beautiful ceremony. Wild flowers everywhere! It was a very happy day. We got many licks on our noses that day. We exchanged diamond studded collars.

That evening, we danced the night away to the band, Boneafide Dogs. There was a lot of paw shaking and howling going on. Tail wagging and dog butt wiggling were everywhere. We got many biscuits and dog chews as gifts. Yum!

Love means knowing when to lead and knowing when to follow. We are like two peas in a pod. We enjoy many of the same things. We both love chasing our own tails. We like getting dirty digging holes in the yard to bury dog bones. We love going for walks with our human owners.

HONEYMOON

POOPSY

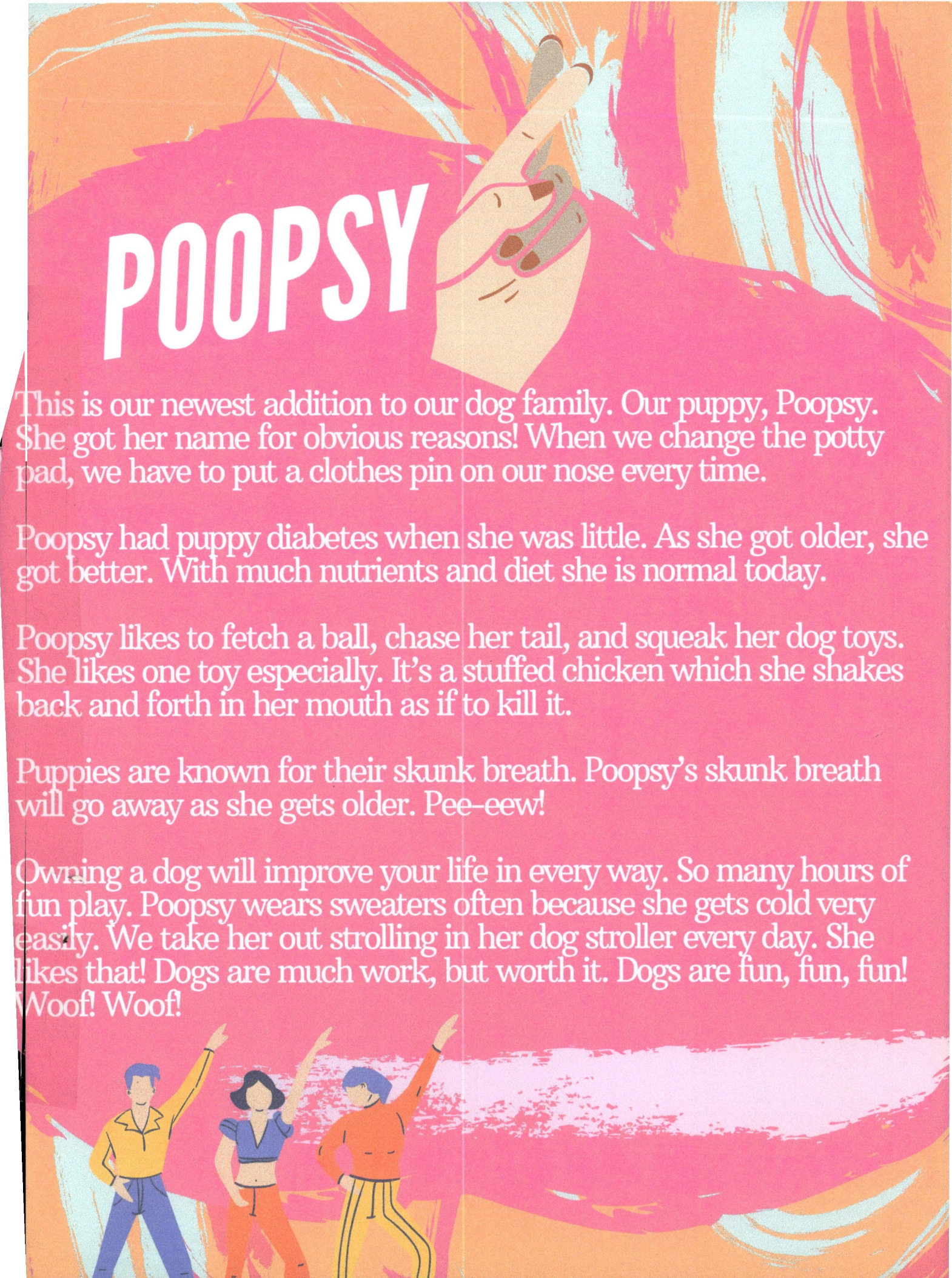

This is our newest addition to our dog family. Our puppy, Poopsy. She got her name for obvious reasons! When we change the potty pad, we have to put a clothes pin on our nose every time.

Poopsy had puppy diabetes when she was little. As she got older, she got better. With much nutrients and diet she is normal today.

Poopsy likes to fetch a ball, chase her tail, and squeak her dog toys. She likes one toy especially. It's a stuffed chicken which she shakes back and forth in her mouth as if to kill it.

Puppies are known for their skunk breath. Poopsy's skunk breath will go away as she gets older. Pee–eew!

Owning a dog will improve your life in every way. So many hours of fun play. Poopsy wears sweaters often because she gets cold very easily. We take her out strolling in her dog stroller every day. She likes that! Dogs are much work, but worth it. Dogs are fun, fun, fun! Woof! Woof!

www.ingramcontent.com/pod-product-compliance
Lightning Source LLC
Chambersburg PA
CBHW051629140626
46547CB00033B/2945